YOUNG RESEARCHER

THE EGYPTIANS

Stuart Fleming

First published in 1992 by
Heinemann Children's Reference,
a division of Heinemann Educational Books Ltd,
Halley Court, Jordan Hill, Oxford OX2 8EJ.

OXFORD   LONDON   EDINBURGH
MADRID   PARIS   ATHENS   BOLOGNA
MELBOURNE   SYDNEY   AUCKLAND   SINGAPORE
TOKYO   IBADAN   NAIROBI   GABORONE   HARARE
PORTSMOUTH NH (USA)

Designed by Julian Holland Publishing Ltd
Picture Research by Ann-Marie Ehrlich
Colour artwork by Gecko and Martin Smillie
Editorial planning Jackie Gaff

Printed in Hong Kong

British Library Cataloguing in Publication Data

Fleming, Stuart
    The Egyptians. – (Young researcher)
    I. Title II. Series
    932

    ISBN 0-431-00570-2

Photographic acknowledgements

The authors and publishers wish to acknowledge with thanks, the following photographic sources:
a = above b = below l = left r = right
By courtesy of the Trustees of the British Museum 23*l*, 31*r*, 33*l*, 36; C M Dixon 9, 21, 22, 24, 25*r*, 28*r*, 31*l*, 35, 37-39, 51*l*, 52, 54, 58; E T Archive 10, 12, 27*a*, 55, 56; Werner Forman Archive 8, 14, 26, 27*b*, 28*l*, 42*l*, 44, 48*r*, 49, 50, 53*l*; Michael Holford 5, 7, 13, 17*l*, 18, 20, 23*r*, 25*l*, 29, 34, 40*l*, 41, 43, 45, 46*l*, 48*l*, 51*r*, 54*br*, 57*l*, 59; Hutchison Library 6, 30, 40*r*, 46*r*; William Macquitty 11*l*, 17*r*, 33*r*, 42*r*, National Center for Supercomputing Applications 11*r*
The publishers have made every effort to trace the copyright holders, but if they have inadvertently overlooked any, they will be pleased to make the necessary arrangement at the first opportunity.

Note to the reader
In this book there are some words in the text which are printed in **bold** type. This shows that the word is listed in the glossary on page 62. The glossary gives a brief explanation of words which may be new to you.

Contents

Who were the Egyptians?

About 5000 years ago, a remarkable way of life, or **civilization**, grew up along the banks of the River Nile in Egypt. It flourished for over 3000 years, longer than any other civilization in the world's history. It produced Egypt's great pyramids and temples, which filled visitors with wonder. They still fill us with wonder today, for much of ancient Egypt can still be seen. So many buildings and objects have been preserved that experts find it easier to have first-hand knowledge of the Egyptians than of the Greeks or the Romans, even though Egypt is much older. In the following pages you too will have the chance to know what the Egyptians were like.

Who were these people that you are about to meet? They are to some extent the same people as the

▽ **A mixture of peoples.** Egypt's original population was drawn to the fertile Nile Valley from the surrounding lands. Later, foreign traders, and also foreign soldiers called mercenaries, who were paid to fight for Egypt, were allowed by the Egyptians to settle. The descendants of slaves and prisoners of war also became Egyptian. Sometimes, for more than 100 years at a time, foreign conquerors ruled Egypt. Many descendants of the foreign armies, officials and servants remained in Egypt when foreign rule ended.

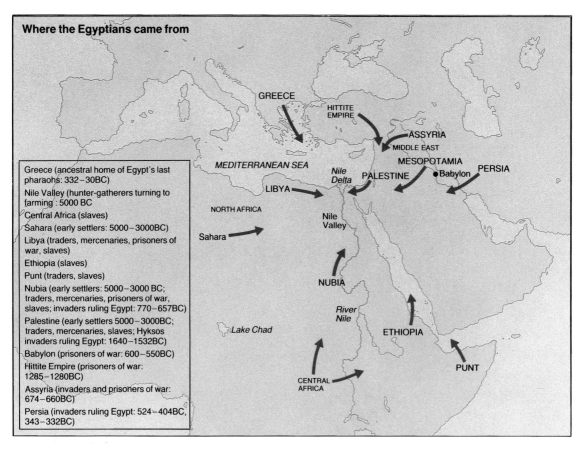

Where the Egyptians came from

Greece (ancestral home of Egypt's last pharaohs: 332–30BC)

Nile Valley (hunter-gatherers turning to farming : 5000 BC)

Central Africa (slaves)

Sahara (early settlers: 5000–3000BC)

Libya (traders, mercenaries, prisoners of war, slaves)

Ethiopia (slaves)

Punt (traders, slaves)

Nubia (early settlers: 5000–3000 BC; traders, mercenaries, prisoners of war, slaves; invaders ruling Egypt: 770–657BC)

Palestine (early settlers 5000–3000BC; traders, mercenaries, slaves; Hyksos invaders ruling Egypt: 1640–1532BC)

Babylon (prisoners of war: 600–550BC)

Hittite Empire (prisoners of war: 1285–1280BC)

Assyria (invaders and prisoners of war: 674–660BC)

Persia (invaders ruling Egypt: 524–404BC, 343–332BC)

GREECE
HITTITE EMPIRE
ASSYRIA
MIDDLE EAST
MESOPOTAMIA
PERSIA
MEDITERRANEAN SEA
Nile Delta
PALESTINE
•Babylon
LIBYA
NORTH AFRICA
Nile Valley
Sahara
NUBIA
River Nile
ETHIOPIA
Lake Chad
PUNT
CENTRAL AFRICA

◁ **Ancient builders of mysterious monuments.** In ancient times, many of Egypt's great monuments were already a mystery to the Egyptians themselves. The Great Sphinx is the stone guardian of the pyramid behind it, where the pharaoh Khephren was buried about 4500 years ago. No one knows why this guardian was given the head of a man and the body of a lion. The statue was first dug out of the sand and marvelled at by the Egyptians of 2400 years ago, when their pharaoh, Thotmes IV, dreamt that the gods commanded him to build a new temple there.

Egyptians of today. People who now live beside the Nile are descended from those who settled in farming villages there before history began. They are also descended from the foreigners who for thousands of years have arrived and settled in their country. The Egyptians are a truly ancient people.

The early Egyptians

Excavations show that the earliest, **prehistoric,** people who grew food by the Nile lived mainly by hunting for meat and gathering wild plants. They kept only a small number of cattle, sheep or goats and grew a few crops.

Their crops, like their domestic animals, had come to Egypt from the Middle East. The crops were flax, barley and a primitive type of wheat called emmer. These plants did not grow wild in the Nile Valley, and they had first been used for farming in the Middle East. Does this mean that the first Egyptian farmers came originally from the east? Probably some of them did. However, the language, art and the religion that grew up in Egypt were so different from those of the Middle East that many experts believe most of the early farming people were of North African descent.

Dates from long ago
Almost all of the dates in this book are 'BC' dates, counting the number of years before the birth of Christ. Add the present number of years *since* the birth of Christ to work out how long ago the time was. When dates are given for things that have happened since the birth of Christ, the letters 'AD' appear in front. For example, the tomb of the Egyptian king, or **pharaoh**, Tutankhamon was found in AD1922. When historians are not sure about a date it is printed in this book with a question mark.

The gift of the Nile

No other civilization in the time of the **pharaohs** could rival Egypt's magnificent buildings, its wealth or its long centuries of peace and stability. To a large extent, this is because other civilizations did not have Egypt's main advantage – its great river. As the Greek historian Heroditus remarked 2400 years ago, Egypt was the gift of the Nile.

Feeding eight million

If you were a trader travelling in the Middle East and Egypt 7000 years ago, you would probably say that Egypt showed little promise, compared to Mesopotamia and to the region that was to become Palestine. Mud and pollen deposits tell us that the Nile Valley at that time was mostly still a swamp. Probably fewer than 30 000 people were able to live there by hunting and gathering, on which the Egyptians still depended. Meanwhile, a walled city had already stood for 1000 years at Jericho, in

▽ **Egypt's great river.** Egypt today is still a riverbank land, depending on the Nile for all of its water. Almost no rain falls on the country, which apart from the Nile Valley is dry and uninhabited, like the hills in the background of this scene near Aswan.

Palestine. For 500 years, farmers in Mesopotamia had produced more food and helped their population grow by controlling the floodwaters of their rivers. They used dikes and **irrigation** canals to control the water.

However, the climate everywhere was becoming drier. Less rain was falling far to the south in the African lands that fed water to the Nile. As the level of the river fell, a strip of rich black land emerged along each of its banks. It was this fertile soil, renewed at the end of every summer by muddy waters when the Nile flooded, that enabled Egypt to become great. By the time the Roman Emperor had them counted, about 2000 years ago, eight million Egyptians lived from the produce of the valley. The Nile also helped by making transport and communication a simple matter for Egyptians. You can read about this Nile gift on page 46.

△ **An everlasting gift of water.** After death, wealthy Egyptians hoped for life everlasting in the Underworld, a land of fertile fields − the Fields of Yaru. The fields were surrounded by blue canals like the ones the living Egyptians dug to channel the Nile waters. This scene is from a scroll buried with the high official Nakht.

The Black Land
'The Black Land' was the Egyptians' name for their country, the land along the Nile (shown in dark green on the map) that could grow crops. Its area was roughly 26 500 square kilometres, and it fell into two parts – the higher land in the south and the lower land near the sea. The higher land was called **Upper Egypt**, which included the Nile Valley, between 1 and 17 kilometres wide, as far north as the waterfall known as the first **cataract**. Its most important city was called Thebes. The lower land was called **Lower Egypt**, which included the **delta** of the river and the wide plain around Memphis, its most important city. Since travel across the desert was difficult, the Egyptians could not easily defend most of their isolated **oases** from the Libyans. The Faiyum was the only oasis constantly under Egyptian control. On every side was the 'Red Land' – deserts that were almost uninhabited. They protected the Black Land from invasion. So did the rapids and cataracts south of Egypt on the Nile. Large numbers of the pharaoh's soldiers could move quickly in boats on the river to meet enemies who advanced only slowly across land.

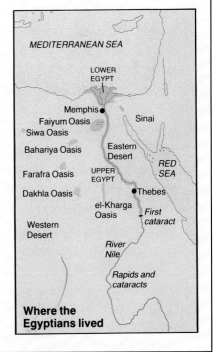

MEDITERRANEAN SEA

LOWER EGYPT

Memphis

Faiyum Oasis
Siwa Oasis

Sinai

Bahariya Oasis

Eastern Desert

RED SEA

Farafra Oasis

UPPER EGYPT

Dakhla Oasis

Thebes

el-Kharga Oasis

First cataract

Western Desert

River Nile

Rapids and cataracts

Where the Egyptians lived

How we know about the Egyptians

About 300 professional **Egyptologists** spend their time at work learning about the Egyptians. They work in universities and museums all over the world, including some in today's Egypt, and at **excavations.** How are they able to piece together a picture of ancient Egyptian life?

Looking beneath the earth

The Egyptians lived in the path of the yearly Nile flood, and their homes were built of mud bricks. The villages stood above the flood on raised parts of the river bank, but over thousands of years the river's banks have eroded many times. All trace of most ancient dwellings has been washed away. Some ruins survive, but lie under present-day villages which **archaeologists** cannot disturb. However, many prehistoric dwelling places, from the days when people lived on the edge of the desert, have been excavated. So have several villages used by tomb builders in the desert.

It is the tombs themselves, however, that make Egyptian archaeology so exciting. The Egyptians believed that a dead person's soul still needed the dead body and special objects buried with it in order to survive after death. They knew that the dry desert preserves things well, and they chose burial places there that are often well preserved today.

Important Egyptians were wealthy enough to build magnificent tombs and furnish them richly with treasures, **inscriptions**, paintings and statues. These give us a much more detailed picture of the past than we can get from burial places in other countries of the time. The people of these countries had less elaborate beliefs than the Egyptians about what a soul would need in the **afterlife**.

We have this detailed picture of Egypt in spite of the fact that tomb robbers were at work whenever

△ **Well preserved by Egypt's dry climate,** this wooden statue from the tombs at Sakkara — probably a priest — is more than 4400 years old. In wetter countries, most wooden objects made so long ago have rotted away. All that has been lost here is the paint that originally covered the statue.

there was warfare or poor law and order in the country. Only a small part of the original funeral treasures still remained by the time archaeology began about 150 years ago.

Looking at stones and papers

Other rich archaeological sites in Egypt are its ancient temples. Egyptian **pharaohs** lived in palaces of mud, but the gods were housed in dwellings of stone. Many temples still stand, with inscriptions and sculptures that tell us about Egyptian beliefs and about achievements of great pharaohs.

We also know about Egypt through thousands of fragments of **papyrus** letters and documents, usually fragments of **scrolls**, that have survived in Egypt's dry air. The writings of foreign travellers who visited Egypt in ancient times also help us.

△ **The golden mask of Tutankhamon** − an unimportant pharaoh whose burial chamber was the only pharaoh's tomb not raided by robbers before it could be studied. The burial treasures are breath-taking. They show that greater pharaohs must have taken immense wealth with them to their graves.

◁ **Egyptian learning** is known to us through writings on papyrus scrolls. This one has survived since about 650BC. It is a copy of a scroll written 1200 years before, explaining how to calculate the areas of triangles and the slopes of pyramids.

Preserving Egypt's past

In AD1954, near the base of the Great Pyramid of Khufu at Giza in Egypt, **archaeologists** found a sealed chamber containing a perfectly preserved funeral boat built of cedar wood. When the chamber was opened, they smelled an ancient aroma of cedar as they breathed air that had been trapped there for 4600 years. The scent and the ancient air that carried it quickly escaped. The archaeologists wondered, if only they could have analysed it, whether they would have discovered that the air had some property that had helped to preserve the boat in such wonderful condition.

In AD1987, an attempt was made to capture some preserved air from a second chamber nearby. Archaeologists carefully drilled a special hole that did not allow air to escape. They lowered a camera into the chamber and were excited to see a second boat. To their disappointment, however, the air samples that they pumped out smelled stale, and they found signs that construction work during the building of a museum at the pyramid had caused damage. Water from a cement mixer had even trickled in, and the second boat was slightly less well preserved.

Scientific archaeology

Stories like this show how difficult it is to study ancient sites and make them available to visitors without destroying the very traces of the past we want to know about. Today, however, the problems are less discouraging than they once were.

In the past, much information was destroyed by the unscientific collection of objects from ancient sites. Up until the AD1880s objects often arrived in museums with no accurate explanations about where they came from or how the Egyptians had left them. To solve this problem, early archaeologists such as

△ **Before photography,** Egyptologists saved crucial information about many tomb paintings by copying them before they faded. This copy of a tomb wall in Thebes was made by Giovanni Belzoni in 1822. The originals of many of the paintings he copied have now crumbled away. Before exploring Egypt, Belzoni had performed as a strongman in English circuses. He sent many treasures to the British Museum.

◁ **Moving a temple out of harm's way,** these workmen carefully cut and lift stonework at Abu Simbel in the Sudan in order to reassemble it beyond the reach of Lake Nasser. The lake was created in the 1960s when a new dam was built at Aswan.

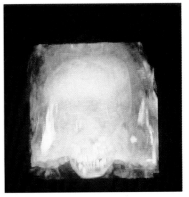

△ **Looking without disturbing.** Scientists used X-rays and computers to make this three-dimensional image of an unknown mummy's head. Mummies do not last long if they are unwrapped, and especially if they are cut open to learn about mummification techniques and causes of death. Much of this information can now be gained by X-raying mummies left undisturbed in their wrappings.

Sir Flinders Petrie taught their students to make very detailed notes at archaeological sites. They recognized that every detail is a clue in the difficult task of piecing together the story of the past.

Another problem is that ancient objects, once unburied, do not last long in the light and the open air. Museums can preserve the objects that are removed. They have special rooms where the moisture, light and temperature are controlled.

Pictures and picture writing

I f you look at paintings in Egyptian tombs, you will sometimes be struck by their lifelessness. You may feel that it must be impossible ever to understand people who had so little expression in their faces, and stood with such strange postures. But the Egyptians were not painting these images to show what people were really like. Instead, a picture was a kind of diagram, thought to have magical power. For example, the painting of Nakht harvesting, on page 7, was made as a charm, to help this dead nobleman's spirit feed itself in the **afterlife**.

◁ **Pictures like writing.** In this inscription on a funeral stone from Abydos in Egypt, the artist has followed just as many rules in forming the images of the dead man and his wife as he has in forming the hieroglyphic symbols. As in almost all Egyptian paintings, we see the shoulders as though they are facing us, but we see the rest of the body in profile. The man is facing right. Any figure and any hieroglyphic symbol does this unless there is a special reason for facing left. When two people face each other, it is the inferior who faces left. The symbols above the two figures face right, as can be seen from the duck's head, bottom left in the third column. For symmetry, the symbols by the woman face left, as can be seen from the hawk near her foot.

To preserve the magical power of their art, the Egyptians believed they must copy exactly the style handed down through the ages. This meant that most artists painted in the same way, and the people they painted all looked the same. Some images that occur again and again — for example, the human face — are almost as unchanging in their style as the letters in an alphabet.

In fact, tomb pictures were closely connected with Egypt's famous picture writing, or **hieroglyphics**, invented about 5000 years ago (around 3000BC). The Egyptians believed hieroglyphics were magical too, and they used them mostly in temples and tombs.

Misleading images

Some tomb pictures show Egyptian dancing and sports, but the topics of most images and hieroglyphic **inscriptions** make Egyptians seem like a very solemn people who thought about hardly anything but life after death, gods and making war on enemies. However, the thousands of fragments that remain of everyday **papyrus** letters, official reports and essays give a very different impression.

Many of the writings tell us that Egyptians, like anyone else, told jokes, complained, quarrelled and sometimes behaved badly. Thieves robbed the living as well as the dead in their tombs, and judges sometimes took bribes, or dishonest payments to let the thieves go. Ambitious officials and generals plotted against their pharaohs. Discontented soldiers, peasants and slaves ran away from their masters.

These ordinary writings were in **hieratic script**, which did not use pictures and could be written more quickly than hieroglyphics. About 2700 years ago, the Egyptians created an even simpler form of writing called **demotic script**.

Horus   b-j-k (hawk)

△ **Spelling it out.** All hieroglyphic symbols began as pictures standing for whole words, such as this hawk, the symbol of the god Horus. To write all the words they wanted to, however, the Egyptians needed to put some word pictures to work as signs for sounds — the signs spelling the word 'hawk', for example, which was pronounced "bejek".

△ **The Rosetta Stone,** named after the Nile Delta town of Rashid, where it was found in AD1799. The inscription was carved during the Greek period in hieroglyphics (top), demotic script (middle) and Greek (bottom). Working from his knowledge of Greek, the French scholar Jean François Champollion used the stone in the AD1820s to become the first man for more than a thousand years to read ancient Egyptian writing.

Egypt's pharaoh kings

We get the word **pharaoh** from two Egyptian words 'per aa', meaning 'great house' or 'palace'. 'Pharaoh' means simply 'the one who lives in the palace'. The pharaohs also had a long list of more official titles.

The Egyptians believed that no single name could express the greatness of their ruler. They thought he was more than human and addressed him with the names of several gods. You will learn about these divine titles on page 16.

The Egyptians also addressed the pharaoh with titles that combined Upper Egyptian and Lower Egyptian words for 'king'. In this way they expressed the idea that he held their country together.

The royal dynasties

A pharaoh usually had several wives. One of them was his 'great royal queen', who was believed to have the special blessing of Isis, the mythical first goddess-queen of Egypt, and Hathor, the goddess of women.

Historians think that it was the custom to make the great royal queen's eldest son, who was not necessarily the eldest of all the sons of the pharaoh, the heir to the throne. If the great queen had only a daughter, a son of one of the pharaoh's other wives might marry this daughter, his half-sister.

Sometimes a nobleman who was not a son of the pharaoh married her. The daughter's husband became pharaoh when her father died, and she became the great royal queen.

A line of rulers, passing on their throne from one member of their family to another over the generations, is called a **dynasty**. Over 3000 years, many Egyptian dynasties died out or were overthrown by foreign conquerors or Egyptian plots. In all, 31 dynasties ruled the Egyptians.

△ **Before the first pharaohs,** many kings fought for control of different parts of the Nile Valley. In this predynastic carving, King Narmer, wearing the crown of Upper Egypt, kills a captive enemy.

| Crown of Upper Egypt | Crown of Lower Egypt | Crown of all Egypt | War crown | Hemhemet crown |

The pharaohs of 3000 years

Egyptologists try to work out when particular pharaohs ruled and when particular dynasties began and ended by studying ancient Egyptian historians' own lists. Some ancient scrolls mention comets and the positions of stars and planets during the reign of particular pharaohs. Today's knowledge of astronomy tells us when certain heavenly events, like the appearance of a comet, must have happened, and so it tells us more precisely when these pharaohs ruled.

Egyptian dynasties are grouped by periods. The three most oustanding periods are called kingdoms. The times before there were pharaohs are called the **predynastic period.** They are followed by the **early period**, the time of the first pharaohs. Three **intermediate periods** were times of civil war. The **late period** and the **Greek period** were times of foreign domination.

	Years before Christ (BC)	Dynasties
Predynastic period	5000 - 3100?	
Early period	3100 - 2649?	1 - 2
Old Kingdom (about 500 years)	**2649 - 2134?**	**3 - 8**
1st intermediate period	2134 - 2040?	9 - 11
Middle Kingdom (about 400 years)	**2040 - 1640?**	**11 - 14**
2nd intermediate period	1640 - 1550?	15 - 17
New Kingdom (about 500 years)	**1550 - 1070?**	**18 - 20**
3rd intermediate period	1070 - 712?	21 - 25
Late period	712 - 332	25 - 31
Greek period	332 - 30	31

△ **Crowns of the pharaohs.** On some occasions a pharaoh wore the white crown of Upper Egypt, on others the red crown of Lower Egypt. Often he wore a combined crown to symbolize the country's unity. In battle, he wore the blue war crown. He wore the full *hemhemet* crown only for certain temple ceremonies. It was more common to wear just the royal headcloth, forming the bottom part of the hemhemet crown.

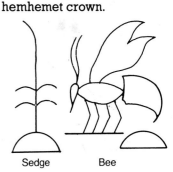

Sedge   Bee

△ **Two words for 'king'.** To symbolize the unity of Egypt, the pharaoh's official title included the words *nisut* ('sedge' — the Lower Egyptian symbol of royalty) and *bity* ('bee' — the Upper Egyptian symbol). These are the hieroglyphic signs for the words.

The pharaohs and the gods

The Egyptians addressed their pharaoh as though he were a god, and not just one god, but several. His official title included the name of the hawk-headed god Horus. He was also called 'Golden Horus', which was like saying 'Horus, who is made of the same precious substance as Re, the sun-god'. Re was the country's chief god. The pharaoh's title had phrases like 'son of Re' and 'giver of life like Re'.

The pharaoh was also called by the name of the vulture goddess Nakhbet, protectress of **Upper Egypt,** and by the name of the cobra goddess Wadjet, protectress of **Lower Egypt**. When he died, yet another title was inscribed on a pharoah's tomb. This was Osiris, the name of the god who ruled the **Underworld**, the place where all good Egyptians lived after death.

The Myth of Osiris

In Egyptian myth, Osiris was god-king of Egypt until his brother Seth cut Osiris's body into pieces and scattered the pieces up and down the Nile, in order to seize the country for himself. Osiris's goddess-queen Isis found the pieces and put Osiris back together. He then became the ruler of the Underworld. Horus, the

▽ **The title of Thotmes IV in hieroglyphics.**

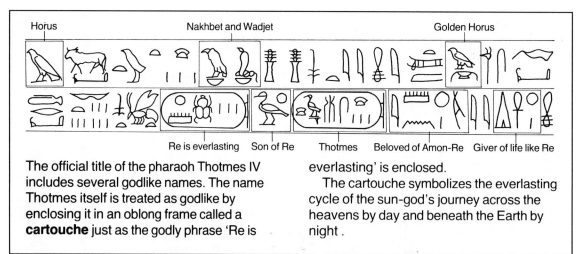

Horus   Nakhbet and Wadjet   Golden Horus

Re is everlasting   Son of Re   Thotmes   Beloved of Amon-Re   Giver of life like Re

The official title of the pharaoh Thotmes IV includes several godlike names. The name Thotmes itself is treated as godlike by enclosing it in an oblong frame called a **cartouche** just as the godly phrase 'Re is everlasting' is enclosed.

The cartouche symbolizes the everlasting cycle of the sun-god's journey across the heavens by day and beneath the Earth by night .

son of Osiris and Isis, fought with Seth for the throne of Egypt. The gods approved of Horus's claim to the throne, and he became the rightful king.

By calling their pharaoh Horus, the Egyptians claimed that the gods approved of him as their rightful king. By calling a dead pharaoh Osiris, they expressed the belief that he would continue to rule them when they died and joined him in the Underworld. The names 'Nakhbet' and 'Wadjet', representing Upper and Lower Egypt, were joined together in the pharaoh's title. This underlined the pharaoh's difficult task of keeping both parts of the country together. Some pharaohs' titles also mentioned the gods of powerful cities. For example, part of Thotmes IV's title is the phrase 'beloved of Amon-Re', the chief god of the important town of Thebes.

△ **Giver of life.** The pharaoh's most godlike names were 'son of Re' and 'giver of life like Re'. The Egyptians believed that by serving the gods, the king helped the sun to rise every morning and helped the Nile to flood at the end of each summer. They believed that in return for the offerings of food and water that only the pharaoh could make, the gods would feed the souls of the Egyptians after death. In this image sculpted into a temple wall, Re symbolically hands an *anhk,* the hieroglyphic symbol for life, to the pharaoh.

◁ **Osiris, king of the Underworld,** receiving offerings from a departed soul. The god holds the symbols of his office — a shepherd's crook in his left hand and a thresher's flail in his right. Each living pharaoh, since he was like an Osiris to the living, also had the right to carry the crook and the flail.

The pyramid-builders

I f you visit Egypt, the buildings that will impress
you most are probably the pyramids. All of them
were built to contain the tombs of pharaohs. So far, 46
pyramids have been located and studied by
archaeologists. Others may still be discovered,
lying unfinished or in ruins, under the desert sands.

Leading the world in stonework

One reason why the pyramids are so fascinating is
that the first of them are the earliest buildings ever to
be made by precisely cutting and putting together
great blocks of stone. In stonework, Egypt led the
world for more than 2000 years.

◁ **The Step Pyramid** as it
appears today (left) and as it
would have appeared (below)
4600 years ago. This was the
first pyramid, built for the
pharaoh Zoser by his great
scribe Imhotep.

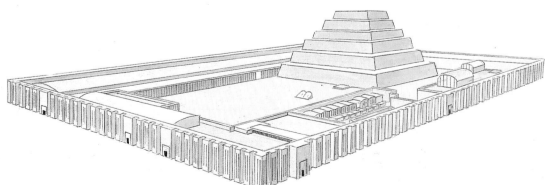

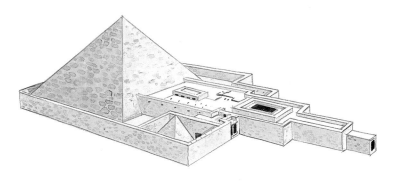

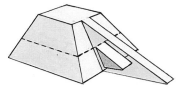

△ **How were the pyramids built?** Probably the work gangs built temporary ramps and hauled the great stones up them over rollers. In some pyramids, each great stone was inscribed with the name of the team that quarried the block, hauled it to the site and put it in place.

△ **A true pyramid,** like this one at Abusir, had smooth sides and came to a point. This is how the pyramid looked when just finished more than 4400 years ago.

Why the pyramids were built

Before the pyramids, pharaohs were entombed in **mastabas,** low rectangular buildings made of bricks or of much smaller stones than those used later in the pyramids. However, in the reign of Zoser (2630-2611?), one of the first pharoahs of the **Old Kingdom,** it was decided to house the pharaoh's everlasting spirit in an everlasting structure. It was also decided that this structure should rise by a series of steps by which the pharaoh's spirit could climb to meet the sun. Other **step pyramids** were started but left unfinished, because the task was too great for later pharaohs of Zoser's **dynasty.** Most pyramids of the next dynasty, the 4th, were given an extra finish that makes them **true pyramids.**

Most pyramids are clustered near the place where Egypt's oldest capital city, Memphis, stood, not far from today's capital, Cairo. During the **Middle Kingdom,** only a few pyramids were built, further south. Near the **New Kingdom** capital of Thebes you will find not pyramids but the Valley of Kings, where the later pharaohs were buried in tombs cut into a rock cliff-face.

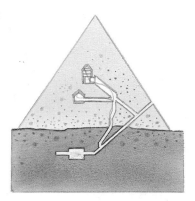

△ **Inside a pyramid,** there was mostly stone or rubble, but also a passageway leading to the pharaoh's burial chamber. In the Great Pyramid of Khufu at Giza, seen here, there were three passageways leading to three chambers. This may have been an attempt to confuse tomb robbers, but it is more likely that Khufu revised the plans for his pyramid as the years of building went by. He found the wealth to make his resting place more and more impressive.

19

Death and the afterlife

The Egyptians believed that at the end of every day, the sun-god Re aged and died in the western sky. But all Egypt prayed for his return so that the crops would continue to grow. In the morning he appeared as though reborn in the east. At the end of every year, under the searing sun, the Nile Valley died. All Egypt prayed for a flood. The flood came and the Earth sprang back to life.

The Egyptians thought that the sun and the valley both survived terrible changes because of a power of the gods to overcome death and decay. When Re died each evening, he descended into an afterlife that was called simply 'the West' during the **Old Kingdom**, and later the **Underworld**. The Underworld was a place of perfection that brought Re back to life as he journeyed through it each night. The Egyptians believed that they too could reach this world if their bodies were preserved.

△ **Funeral ceremonies** included a symbolic opening of the mummy's mouth with a specially shaped stick, so that he could eat in the afterlife. Here four priests perform the ceremony while women weep. The priest holding the mummy plays the role of Anubis, the god of mummification. Anubis had the head of a jackal, the dog-like desert animal that dug unprotected bodies out of the sand and ate them. By making the jackal a god, the Egyptians hoped to turn its power over dead bodies to their favour.

◁ **The judgement of the gods.** Anubis measures the weight of a dead man's heart — where the Egyptians thought life's decisions were made — against the weight of a feather — symbolic of truth. A group of gods is seated above them to pass judgement. If the heart and the feather do not balance, a monster will be summoned by the gods to devour the dead man's soul.

Preserving a home for a spirit

The Egyptians thought that making a **mummy** of a dead person's body, and keeping it in a dry, unchanging condition, gave a lasting home to the person's **ka**, or body-spirit. The *ka* was nourished by Osiris, king of the dead. The dead person also had a winged soul, the **ba**, which was free to move through the Underworld and return to earth, so long as the *ka* survived.

The Egyptians mummified their pharaohs and built them magnificent unchanging tombs of stone. Wealthy and powerful Egyptians also arranged to be mummified and entombed. The paintings, inscriptions and treasures that were entombed with mummies were charms. Their purpose was to help the *ba* overcome hazards on its journey to the Underworld and help it live a pleasant life there.

Later Egyptians came to believe that they all had a chance for at least a humble life after death if they were loyal subjects of the pharaoh, who became like Osiris after he died. Even if he could not afford to be mummified, an obedient person could still hope that his *ba* would join the 'boat of millions', the golden ship full of good souls in which Re crossed the sky.

△ **A tombstone inscription,** like this one, was usually a reminder to the living that on behalf of the dead they should make offerings to Osiris, the king of the Underworld. The offerings requested are 'bread, beer, oxen, fowl, clothing and all things good and pure on which a god lives'.

◁ **Hathor, goddess of women and trees** pours water to quench the thirst of a dead woman's *ka* (body-spirit) and the same woman's *ba* (winged soul). Only if the living fed the gods with offerings, the Egyptians believed, could the gods feed the spirits and the souls of the dead.

Mummies and medicines

The Egyptians thought the dead needed their bodies just as much as the living did. The soul, according to Egyptian religion, needed its physical home. The work of caring for bodies was the work of priests. The priests would make a dead body into a **mummy**, and they would also serve as doctors and surgeons to the living. Making mummies helped them to learn about **anatomy**, and this gave them ideas about how the body works. However, medical science did not make much progress in the 3000 years that the Egyptians practised it.

Visiting the doctor

Papyrus scrolls tell us that treatments for illness involved sacrifices to gods, reciting spells and

▽ **Natural mummification.** The desert sand dried and preserved this Egyptian about 5000 years ago. The clay pots were put into the grave to provide the dead person with useful objects in the next life. The Egyptians took natural mummification as a sign from the gods that preservation of the body was necessary for life after death.

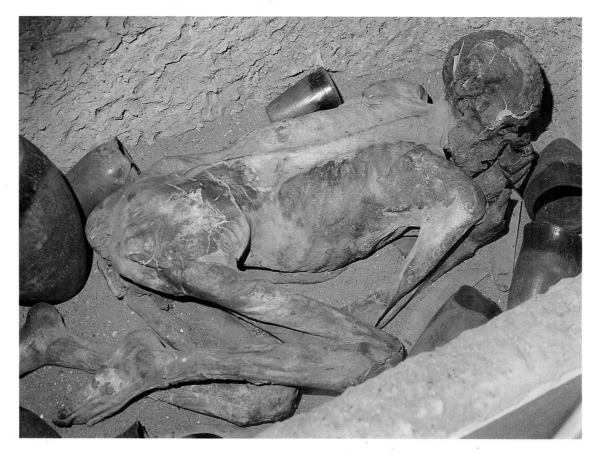

wearing charms. A priest might diagnose your illness as a harmful trick played on you by a dead relative who was annoyed with you. Then he would help you write a letter begging this departed person to leave you alone. Some priest-doctors could also set broken bones very skilfully, and dress wounds. All of them prescribed medicines.

What the Egyptians taught visitors

The Greeks learned many Egyptian remedies and passed them on to the Arabs and medieval Europe — for example, castor oil for constipation. Many strange and useless Egyptian remedies were among them. Imagine taking medicines such as fly dung and the blood of mice! Medieval physicians even added a peculiar one of their own based on ground Egyptian mummy. Swallowing this expensive powder was supposed to cure you of almost any disease.

A small number of Egyptian scrolls give medical explanations for why people become ill. They say that good medicines cure people by repairing the organs that are not working properly. However, the Egyptians did not have any method of discovering the effects of particular medicines on particular organs.

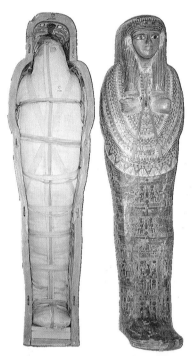

△ **Artificial mummification.** Priests covered the body in natron — a chemical from salt lakes in the desert — for 40 days. The natron drew water out of the body. They wrapped the mummy in linen bandages, often with jewellery inside. This mummy of a priestess of Thebes was put in her carefully painted coffin about 3000 years ago.

◁ **Mummified internal organs,** preserved in 'canopic jars', were put in the tomb along with the mummy. Left to right, the jars contain the dead person's liver, stomach, intestines and lungs. The priests returned the heart to the body before wrapping the mummy. They did not preserve the brain, which they thought was one of the least important parts of the body.

Temples and their gods

The names of over 2000 gods have been found in Egyptian writings. A few are names of gods who were worshipped in the home. Most are names of minor spirits who, local people believed, controlled a particular hill or a particular tree. At that place local people would build a small dwelling of reed matting or mud bricks. This would be a home on Earth, or **shrine**, for the spirit. They would put a clay image inside and pray for the spirit to come into the image, so they could offer sacrifices and ask favours. A few gods were great spirits worshipped throughout a region or throughout the entire land of Egypt. Their images, made by the best craftsmen, were housed in golden shrines kept in stone temples.

Honouring the gods

In many temples, the priests shaved all the hair from their bodies in order to be especially clean for the gods. They also bathed in a sacred pool that was part of the temple complex. The ordinary priests, who might do no more than sweep the temple, were not allowed to look inside the inner sanctuary. Here, behind a clay seal made on the sanctuary door every night, was a golden shrine where a beautiful stone or golden statue was supposed to be inhabited by the god of the temple. Every morning, the priests broke the seal to bring the god out for worship.

Few priests were considered pure enough to attend the worship. Ordinary people were not allowed beyond the temple forecourt. They also worshipped at mud-brick shrines outside. On certain festival days, however, the official shrine was taken out of the inner sanctuary. The god was carried in procession on a miniature Nile boat about three metres long. Ordinary people could see the shrine but not the god inside.

Few women became priestesses, but the

△ **Amon-Re** — the sun-god in the form of Amon, the god of Thebes. This statue, almost 3000 years old, is made of solid silver overlaid with gold.

◁ **Ruins of the temple of Amon at Karnak,** near Thebes. It has been described as the greatest building ever constructed. These columns, which once supported the roof, are so huge that 100 men could stand on the top of each. In the Old and Middle Kingdoms, temples had only part-time priests, serving one month in four. They were scribes or local landholders. In the New Kingdom, the pharaohs gave huge estates to certain temples, so that they could afford magnificent buildings and large numbers of permanent, full-time priests. The temples of Amon at Luxor and Karnak were especially rich.

△ **Animal-headed images** of gods, such as this baboon-headed god and this hare-headed god, expressed the Egyptian belief that particular animals were closely connected with supernatural powers. Many temples were devoted to animals, especially the cat, that were considered sacred. People paid for an animal's burial as a good deed.

high-priestess of Amon was the most holy person in the whole Theban area apart from the pharaoh. She was considered the bride of Amon, and could not marry.

Gods of the pharaohs

In the time before the pharaohs, the **predynastic period**, each region along the Nile had its own ideas about the sun-god, or the king of the dead or the god of creation. It also had its own names for these gods. This meant that there were many different beliefs in Egypt. In an attempt to make a single religion for Egyptians, the pharaohs joined the names of similar gods into one. At different times, depending on which towns in Egypt were most powerful, the pharaohs called the sun-god, for example, Re, Re-Harakhty or Amon-Re.

How Egypt was governed

The governments of countries today have to follow laws that limit their power, but the pharaoh of Egypt was an **absolute ruler**. He did not have to obey any laws himself and he could change as he liked any of the laws that other Egyptians obeyed. However, to rule well, the pharaoh needed help and approval from other people. He needed approval because a pharaoh's reign would be difficult if important people such as the priests, the generals, the highest government officials and the great landholders thought that he was offending the gods. They might think the pharaoh was offending the gods if he changed customs that they liked or if he failed to look after the country's needs. The priests would be less likely to interpret omens of the future and of the gods' wishes in ways that gave people confidence in the pharaoh. When there was little confidence in the pharaoh, local officials became very powerful and ruled independently.

The pharaoh needed help in ruling because he could not be everywhere, deciding every question of government for himself. The pharaoh had to allow other people to act for him, deciding what his wishes were in matters he had not even thought about. Most of his decisions were made by **scribes**. These record-keepers and administrators were strongly influenced by custom and tradition.

△ **Using their laps for writing tables,** scribes like this ran Egypt from mud-brick offices in small villages along the Nile. They collected taxes, settled legal disputes, served as priests, recruited and led armies if the pharaoh needed them, and designed and organized the construction of public buildings.

Scribes, priests and generals

The younger sons of landholding and noble families were trained as scribes. The most privileged of them attended the great school for scribes at Thebes. There they learned history, poetry, surveying, architecture and accountancy, and most went into the pharaoh's service as government officials.

Up until the time of the **New Kingdom**, scribes in the pharaoh's service were very powerful. In the **Old**

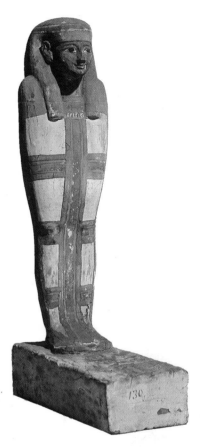

▷ **Standing ready to serve,** this *shabty* figure was buried in a rich man's tomb to do whatever work the gods of the Underworld might command from his master, for the gods levied taxes in the Underworld in the same way that the pharaohs did in life. A living Egyptian would pay his taxes to the pharaoh by sending peasants to work on the pharaoh's projects — anything from repairing canals each year after the flood to building a temple — and by sending grain and other produce to the pharaoh's storehouses. The Egyptians did not use money.

Kingdom the country was divided into provinces, called **nomes** by ancient Greek historians, with 22 in **Upper Egypt** and 20 in **Lower Egypt**. The **nomarch** who governed each nome was usually a scribe of noble birth. **Middle Kingdom** pharaohs thought the nomarchs were too powerful, and so they abolished the nomes. However, they replaced them with larger regions, whose scribes often became powerful. The pharaoh's closest advisers were scribes belonging to the most influential families, and one, the **vizier**, acted as prime minister. During the New Kingdom, however, the closest advisers were full-time generals and full-time priests of the most important temples, who passed their positions on from father to son.

Women in government

Very few women learned to read and write in ancient Egypt, but the Egyptians had a feminine word for scribe. We know very little about women scribes.

In the **Greek period**, numerous Greek-speaking queens called Arsinoe, Bernice or Cleopatra ruled the country, by themselves or with their husbands.

Even before the Greeks, Egypt was ruled at least three times by women: Nefrusobk (1787 - 1783BC?) in the **Middle Kingdom**, Hatshepsut (1473 - 1458BC?) and Twosre (1198 - 1196BC?) in the **New Kingdom**. Of these, probably only Hatshepsut dominated her advisers. Nefertiti, the great royal queen of the New Kingdom pharaoh Akhnaton, took a very active role in his reign (1353 - 1335BC?).

△ **Cleopatra VII,** the last Greek-speaking queen.

Dress and appearance

Egypt is a hot country, and the Egyptians, especially the men, wore few clothes. What they did wear, however, mattered a great deal. It showed how wealthy they were and what their position was in society.

Men usually wore only a **kilt** of light **linen**. This does not mean that all men looked the same. The linen might be good or poor quality. The kilt might be cut roughly like a peasant's and tucked up between the legs to leave them free for stretching and reaching, or it might be long and full like a priest's. The kilt could be knotted elaborately at the waist. This showed that the man was not ordinary, because such a knot would be impractical for someone who was doing physical work.

△ **A high official and his wife** look simply dressed in this painted limestone statue of about 2550BC. However, the cloth is of the highest quality, and the man's necklace is a sign of rank. So is his long, plaited hair. Men are usually painted red in Egyptian art. Women are often a paler colour, suggesting that women thought it was unfeminine to go out in the sun as much as men.

◁ **Older children wore their hair in a sidelock,** like these two boys of Old Kingdom times. Most children wore no clothing, but jewellery such as these boys' necklaces, and hair carefully groomed by servants, showed when a child's family was wealthy. The heads of the youngest children, even the girls, were shaved bald. An advantage of this was that they were free from head lice.

How women dressed

Women's clothing was also made of linen. Everyday wear for a peasant woman might be of rough, unbleached linen. Wealthy women wore only light, fine linen woven from best-quality thread. It was usually bleached white, but might be dyed orange, yellow or green. Best dresses were pleated.

Cosmetics and hairstyle

Women wore eye make-up, lip paint and rouge for the cheeks when they wanted to look their best. Favourite colours for highlighting the eyes were black and green. These colours symbolized fertility and new life after death. On formal or festive occasions, men used eye make-up to give their eyes the heavy outline that is so common in Egyptian paintings.

Women almost always wore their hair long. However, for the woman who could afford one, the addition of an elaborate wig was considered important when she wanted to be especially attractive to a man. The wig was made of human hair traded to a wig-maker by poor women.

△ **Priestly robes** for a man and his wife making offerings to the gods. The linen is so finely woven that you can see through it. A less formal dress for a man would have short sleeves and reach only to his knees. The woman wears a cone of animal fat on top of her wig. The fat, gradually melting into the hair, is scented with a strong perfume.

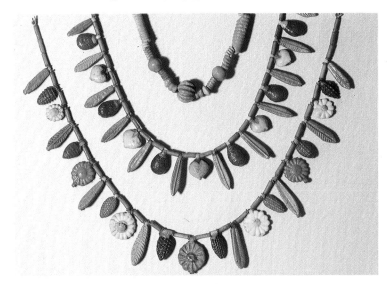

◁ **Glazed ceramic jewellery** from 2500 years ago, was everyday wear for a wealthy woman. Peasant women wore beads too, but theirs were of poorer quality. On formal occasions, wealthy women wore lotus flowers, and rings, earrings, necklaces, bracelets and anklets made of silver, gold and precious stones. Gold was used more than silver. Some beautiful objects were worn as much for magic as for decoration. Rings and brooches in the shape of powerful symbols were used for warding off evil.

An Egyptian village

If you visited a village in ancient Egypt, you would glimpse it first from a boat, because there were no roads at that time. After mooring your boat, you would probably come first to a market place. Unless the village was very important it is unlikely that it had a market every day, and this space might not be very busy when you arrived. In the narrow lanes leading off the market, you would see the two-room or three-room houses of ordinary people. Most of the men might be away working in the fields behind the village. If there were marshes nearby, many residents would be herdsmen who went there to tend cattle, sheep, goats or pigs. However, craftsmen worked in their homes, and many of the women of the village would spend much of the day indoors weaving linen.

You would meet small naked children running and playing in the street. Older boys would be labouring in the fields or in their fathers' workshops. Girls

▽ **A present-day village** near Luxor stands on a hillside behind ancient statues of pharaohs. A typical village in ancient times would be a similar group of flat-roofed buildings, but close together, because most villages were among the fields, on a raised part of the canal bank or riverbank. Very little of the valuable farmland could be spared for space between buildings. Almost all Egyptians lived in communities of about this size. There were no large towns. Apart from Memphis and Thebes, there were no small towns.

The village market

If you visited even a small village on market day, you would probably hear the market from some distance before you arrived. People from several villages upriver and downriver would be thronging the market place, and there would be noisy trading for the goods that local craftsmen and local peasant women laid out on cloths on the ground.

Most trade would be in simple foodstuffs, such as salt, barley, onions, peas and beans. There would also be freshly baked barley bread, ready to eat on the spot, and clay jugs of sour-smelling beer. You would probably be taken aback by the strong aroma of Nile fish, offered fresh, salted and dried.

You would also find cloth, leather, woven baskets and clay pots. There might be some jewellery. Probably two or three travelling magicians would be selling medical advice and charms for protection against evil. In a small market, you would probably not find many luxury goods.

△ **A village house.** This clay model found in a tomb, shows a craftsman's house with living quarters above and workshops on the ground floor. Archaeologists know very little about Egyptian villages. They were made of mud bricks, and thousands of years of flooding have destroyed all traces of most of them.

would be weaving. You might also meet people leading donkeys through these lanes, carrying burdens. Dogs and pigs might be seen sniffing through kitchen rubbish that had been thrown out of doorways. The smells of the neighbourhood would include beer brewing, onions in cooking pots, and urine, used by the leather-maker to soak hair from animal hides.

Landholders and senior government scribes had large homes surrounded by walls on the edges of villages, or standing apart from them.

◁ **A village market scene.** Few villagers could afford meat, but in those markets that had it, the beef was fresh. It was killed and cut up on the spot.

Inside the home

Very few Egyptian homes have been excavated. The floodwaters of the Nile and thousands of years of building and rebuilding on old sites have left nothing of the houses in which people lived by the rivers and canals in ancient times. In the desert near royal tombs, however, workmen and skilled craftsmen were housed in special villages whose remains show us how people lived.

The house of a craftsman

All Egyptian homes were built of mud bricks. In the better ones, including those of skilled craftsmen, the bricks stood on a stone foundation. The interior walls, and even the floors, might be plastered, but in many the floors were simply hard-packed earth.

The houses that have been excavated in the desert opened side by side directly onto the street. They were long and narrow. The front room had a special enclosed platform in one corner, built of mud bricks and reached by a few steps. This was a shrine to the family ancestors. Here the family would leave food and beer for grandfathers and great-grandfathers and ask them to use their influence in the afterlife on behalf of the family. In some homes, there was a

▽ **Inside a craftsman's home** at Deir el-Medina near Thebes, where a village was built 3500 years ago for workers making and furnishing the royal tombs nearby. Unlike most villages, this one was in the desert, which preserved many of its remains.

Roof fence · Vent · Door to bedroom · Palm logs and thatch · Workroom · Mud-brick oven · Open-air kitchen · Birth shrine · Pillar · Shrine · Cellar · Cellar

special bed on this platform, where the children were born. The ancestors in the shrine were supposed to ensure that no wicked souls were born into the family. Small statues of the gods who protected childbirth were also kept there.

A few steps led up to the second room, the main one in the house. It was a raised room with small windows high on the wall letting light in across the roof. In better houses this room had a stone pillar, or at least a palm trunk to support the roof. In the walls there were shrines to gods. There might be a mud bench built into the wall.

If the house was wide enough, two narrower rooms came next. One was likely to be the only bedroom, where people slept on mats on the floor. The other might be a workroom, where a craftsman made pottery or carved wood or women wove linen. A flight of steps at the back of the house led up to the roof, which was fenced off from the neighbouring roofs. This is where the family ate the evening meal. It also provided extra sleeping space. The kitchen too was outdoors, in a yard at the back of the house shaded by a reed thatch.

△ **Bes, god of the household** and protector of women and childbirth. Every home had a shrine with his image in it.

◁ **Bedroom furniture of a wealthy Egyptian.** The tightly woven canvas that would have been stretched taut across the bedframe for a sleeping surface rotted away long ago. The Egyptians used a headrest, seen here on the floor at the rear, instead of a pillow.

Family life

Most of what we know about Egyptian life has been told to us by Egyptian men. It is men who designed the sculptures and wall paintings and wrote the papyrus **scrolls** that we must rely on, and they were mainly concerned with the life men led in the world. There are glimpses, however, of what life was like for the women and the children who stayed at home.

Husbands and wives

Some powerful men, in particular the **pharaoh**, had more than one wife, but this **polygamy** was

▽ **Nebamon and his family** hunting birds in the marshes, a painting in his tomb from about 3400 years ago. Women and children are sometimes shown as tiny figures beside gigantic husbands in Egyptian paintings and sculptures.

The cat – more than a family pet
Cats were considered sacred in Egypt, even those that
wandered free, feeding on the mice that infested granaries.
The male was thought to represent the sun, and the female
to represent the goddess Bast. Both sexes were supposed
to be cherished by the ferocious Sekhmet, a cat-headed
goddess of war. Whole temples were devoted to cat
worship. In the late period, anyone who killed a cat could
become the victim of mob violence. It was forbidden to take
cats out of Egypt. Special commissioners were sometimes
sent to other countries to buy back cats that had been
smuggled away.

△ **The mummy of a cat**
from about 3000 years
ago. The domestic cat
originated in Egypt from
a North African form of
the wildcat. Cats with
collars first appeared in
tomb paintings around
2600BC.

uncommon. Many people died young, however, of
the many diseases that Egyptian medicine could not
effectively treat, and so widows and widowers
frequently remarried. It was very common to have
stepbrothers and stepsisters, as well as half-brothers
and half-sisters.

Egyptian women could own property, unlike the
women of many other civilizations of those times. A
scroll written by the tax assessor for the Faiyum Oasis
in 1156BC shows that about 10 per cent of the land
there belonged to women. It was usual for the wife to
be the person who owned the furnishings in her
husband's house.

The children
In wealthy families, children probably played most of
the day. However, young boys still at home probably
spent some of their time learning to read and write
before being sent away to study in a temple school. In
ordinary families, children had no education. They
worked, the boys alongside their fathers in the fields
or at their fathers' trades, the girls weaving and
cooking and caring for younger children alongside
their mothers.

Entertainment

Adults and children, rich and poor, all Egyptians enjoyed leisure. Peasants had less of it, but they still had time for singing and dancing, and sometimes a special meal. However, most of what we know about Egyptian entertainment is what we see in tomb paintings showing the wealthy. Children play tug-of-war and a kind of leapfrog. Sometimes boys play at soldiers or balance on one another's shoulders. Girls dance in circles and they play catch with brightly coloured balls.

Hunting and boating

Entire families went hunting by boat in the marshes. For a wealthy family, simply sailing on the river was a pleasure. The boat, made of wood (a very scarce material in Egypt), would have a canopy, or covering, to shade the family sitting comfortably near the back of the boat while oarsmen rowed or tended the sails.

When men hunted lions and other large animals in the desert, they left their families at home. Hunting dogs helped them to find and chase their quarry. After horses came to Egypt, about 3500 years ago, they often hunted from horse-drawn chariots.

◁ **A horse on wheels** that has survived for 2000 years since the Roman period. Children's toys included carved monkeys on horseback and wooden dolls. There were wooden cats, leopards and mice with mouths that opened and closed when children pulled a string.

◁ **Playing senet** – Ani, an Egyptian noble, and his wife in a scene painted over 3200 years ago. The rules of senet have been lost, but many boards and their pieces have been found in tombs, where they were left so that the dead could still play. Instead of dice, there were throwsticks to show how many spaces a player could move.

Feasting

Many tomb paintings show banquet scenes where servants offer wine and rich dishes to guests who have cones of animal fat, scented with perfume, on their heads. As the warm evening wears on, the fat melts through each guest's wig and down the neck. The guests take food from the offered dishes with their fingers, which they rinse later when a servant comes with a bowl of water.

◁ **Dancing girls and musicians** entertain banquet guests. Besides handclapping and flute playing, musicians, who were often women, might play harp or lute music, or tap finger drums. We know what all of these instruments would have sounded like, but we do not know the music, for none was ever written down.

Cooking and eating

Egyptian peasants ate mainly barley bread and onions, and they drank a good deal of beer. Occasionally, they could afford to eat fish. From time to time, garlic, green vegetables, dates, figs and other fruit, beans, chickpeas and lentils also helped to vary the diet. However, few Egyptians ever tasted the rich variety of expensive delicacies available to the wealthy.

Food for the rich

The rich could choose from about 40 different varieties of fancy bread, some round, some conical, some plaited. There were breads that contained honey, others that contained milk or eggs. Wheat bread was another luxury, especially when yeast was added to make it rise. About 5000 years ago, Egyptian cooks discovered that if you mix some fresh yeasty beer with a flour ground from unroasted wheat, it can be kneaded into a springy dough that bakes into a high, light loaf.

Cooked meals were sometimes left in tombs for the departed soul. From the remarkably well-preserved remains of one of these meals, prepared almost 5000 years ago, we know that, besides bread, wealthy Egyptians in **predynastic** times were fond of roasted quails, pigeon stew, kidneys, beef ribs, fresh berries, barley cakes and cheese. They might expect all of these in a single fancy meal.

Tomb paintings often show geese being herded past scribes for counting, being plucked and being salted before storage in clay jars. Pigeons liked to nest on Egyptian temples, which reminded them of clifftops. This made them readily available for meat. The Egyptians were very fond of chicken, but this bird did not reach Egypt until the time of the **New Kingdom**.

Game from the Nile marshes, especially raw salted

△ **A servant fans a charcoal cooking fire.** Cooking was in an outdoor kitchen, shaded by reed matting or a thatch of palm leaves. One of the main activities was roasting barley, to crack the outer coverings — the husks. The cracked barley was then ground to release the flour. Barley flour was sometimes boiled as porridge in a clay pot over the fire. More often it was baked as flat round loaves of unleavened, or unrisen, bread in a bee-hive shaped oven.

◁ **Making beer 4400 years ago.** To make beer the Egyptians mashed barley bread into a pot of water, added a small amount of old beer with live yeast in it, and let the mixture stand for about a week. The yeast grew, turning the natural sugars in the barley into alcohol. The remains of the bread were then strained off and the cloudy liquid drunk quickly before it could turn to vinegar. The Egyptians grew grapes and made wine from them, but only for the rich. The grapes were crushed by barefooted peasants treading on them in large vats. Red wines were made from grapes with the skins left on. Greek travellers reported white wines as well, made from grapes with skins removed.

△ **Grinding barley.** This woman of 4000 years ago is pushing a smaller stone back and forth over a stone slab piled with cracked barley. Bits of husk remained in flour produced in this way. X-rays of mummies reveal that even wealthy and royal Egyptians had very worn teeth as a result. This helped to prevent decay, because food does not catch easily in evenly worn teeth.

birds, was a luxury. The marshes also provided luxury vegetables, such as wild celery, **papyrus** stalks and lotus root. Eels, mullet, carp, giant perch, tiger fish and many other fishes were taken from the river and the canals by fishermen in papyrus boats.

The farming year

The Egyptians had three seasons of four months each. The months were all 30 days long, with three ten-day weeks. An extra five days, to make up 365, were added to the calendar as temple festival days between months. From time to time extra days had to be added to make up for the fact that the Egyptians did not have a regular leap year with an extra day every four years as we do. In some periods, this was not done, and their calendar gradually drifted out of harmony with the seasons.

The first season was the time of the flood, called **akhet**. It lasted from August to October. Then came **peret,** the time of planting and fresh growth. This was November to February. March to August was the dry season, called **shemu**, when the crops ripened and were harvested.

The season of the flood

While the brown waters of the Nile flowed across the fields, no farming could be done. Peasants had the time to travel in **papyrus** boats to temples, shrines and distant markets. This was the season when they were most likely to hold village festivals in honour of local spirits. It was also the season when the pharaoh's scribes required landholders to send peasants to work on public projects, such as building pyramids or temples.

△ **Still in use in the twentieth century,** the shaduf (also called the water-sweep) was invented in Mesopotamia and came into use in Egypt about 4000 years ago. Water for crops is lifted out of the river in a goat-skin bag, which swings round onto the bank for emptying.

◁ **Harvesting grain.** Two children looking for fallen grains to take home to their families fight for possession of a prize find. The stalks are being cut with sickles, curved sticks with tiny pieces of sharp flint stuck into them in a row. Blades of copper were better, but too expensive. The cut grain is carried away in baskets to the threshing floor, where oxen treading on the stalks will separate them from the ears.

◁ **Winnowing.** After the threshing, peasants throw the grain in the air so that the chaff, the light outer covering, can blow away in the breeze. Then the grain will be stored in granaries.

Sowing and reaping

Just after the flood came one of the busiest times of the farming year. Men with wooden hoes, or cattle drawing wooden ploughs, turned over the new deposit of soil left by the flood and folded it into the fields.

After scattering the seed for the new crop, the peasants would drive a herd of cattle, goats or pigs over the field. Their hooves pressed the seeds firmly into the ground. The landholder's scribes directed the work and kept records of how much each peasant had done. Lazy workers were beaten.

When the seed was in, time could be found for repairing any damage done by the flood, such as canals that had become blocked with mud left behind by the flood water. Weeding, usually with hoes, was also needed, and water had to be lifted out of the canals to help the fields that had been least moistened by the flood.

While the crop ripened, life became rather relaxed, but the harvest itself was a time of urgency. Peasant women and children, as well as men, worked quickly to finish reaping before the flood covered the fields once again.

Crafts and materials

The tombs of the earliest pharaohs were raided by robbers during later periods of Egyptian history. However, what little remains of the treasures buried with these kings shows that, 5000 years ago, Egyptian craftsmen were producing objects of superb workmanship in stone, copper, gold and wood.

By the reign of Zoser (2630-2611BC?), the first great pharaoh of the **Old Kingdom**, almost all tomb objects were made in the special Egyptian styles that craftsmen were to follow for another 2600 years, and even long into the Roman period. Egyptian style changed very little. It requires expert knowledge to tell whether a piece of jewellery or a statue was made 4500, 3500 or 2500 years ago.

Working with stone

Predynastic **hunter-gatherers** in the Nile Valley produced some of the most finely worked arrowheads and stone tools anywhere in the world during prehistoric times. The farming communities which came after them added pottery, leatherwork and basketweaving to the list of Nile crafts. These ancient farmers hollowed out narrow-necked jars from stone, giving them delicately thin walls. Experts today do not know how they achieved this.

△ **Raised relief,** like this scene of a pharaoh making offerings to the sun-god Re, was a special form of stone sculpture. It was done by cutting away the surface of the stone to a depth of about 5 millimetres from around the figures. The figures were sculpted to stand out from the stone. Raised relief was usually used inside temples. The sun shines directly on this one because the temple is now in ruins.

◁ **Sunk relief,** like this one on the outer wall of a temple at Kom Ombo in southern Egypt, was used outdoors because it shows up better in sunlight. The figures are cut into the stone.

From the earliest days of the Old Kingdom, painted stone statues and **reliefs** were made for temples and pyramids. The craftsmen who made a statue, relief or painting worked in groups to a plan drawn by a senior **scribe** on a papyrus marked in a squared grid to make copying easier. The stone (or plaster in the case of some paintings) was marked into a matching grid and the drawing was copied.

For statues, the grid and the drawing within it were repeatedly cut away as the stone was cut away with copper or bronze tools. The grid and drawing had to be copied onto the stone again and again as the work progressed. Statues and reliefs were always painted, although today much of the paint has worn away. Like the sculptors, craftsmen who painted the sculptures followed a plan on a grid.

▽ **Craftsmanship in metal.** Even in very early times, the Egyptians made excellent copperware, like these pieces from about 2300BC. However, stone was the main material for tools and arrowheads, because metals were in such short supply. Bronze, which is a mixture, or an alloy, of copper and tin, was little used because tin was rare in Egypt. Iron too was rare, and this was unfortunate for the Egyptians. The country's enemies had tougher iron tools and weapons, and in the end they could dominate Egypt. Gold was the only metal that the Egyptians had more of than other countries.

Trade and trade routes

Each Egyptian village produced almost all that was needed in everyday life. There were barley and onions to eat, linen for clothing, mud bricks for building and clay pots for storage. However, the Egyptians liked to trade with each other and with foreigners to get a better variety and quality of goods.

Trade between Egyptians

The Egyptians did not use money. Instead they took something valuable with them to market to **barter** for what they wanted. Papyrus **scrolls** tell us many examples of the bargains that were made. For example, a skilled craftsman might trade a carved walking-stick for a supply of wheat. Traders used metal weights called **deben** to help them judge the value of payments that could be weighed, such as a sack of grain.

You would not find well-made luxury goods in the market-places of most villages. For these, you might have to travel to an important town. It is likely that villages specialized in producing different goods. The best pots would be made in a village that had

▽ **The Queen of Punt** with a procession of men bearing gifts for Hatshepsut, the Queen of Egypt. Hatshepsut's temple near Thebes has several reliefs, like this one, depicting an expedition she sent to the land of Punt, probably present-day Somalia, to trade for frankincense, a scent made from the gum trees that grew there. Frankincense was used in temple rituals. The Queen of Punt had a disease that caused her limbs to swell.

better clay, the best copper knives or the best flint-toothed sickles in another. For special linen, beer or bread, you might have to spend an hour or two travelling on the river.

One luxury food that you would find in most markets was salt. Plant food contains very little salt of the kind we commonly buy for the kitchen today. Since Egyptian peasants ate mostly barley and onions, they probably longed for salt. A great deal of salt was used for preserving fish. The salt came from the Nile Delta, where sea water was trapped in shallow lagoons and left to evaporate. The salt was taken by boat up the Nile and traded.

△ **Hatshepsut's soldiers** carrying herbs from the Land of Punt. Egypt traded with several of the African lands to the south of her. They provided gold and unusual luxuries such as pet baboons. The Egyptians traded many of their African goods, such as frankincense, on to Mediterranean countries.

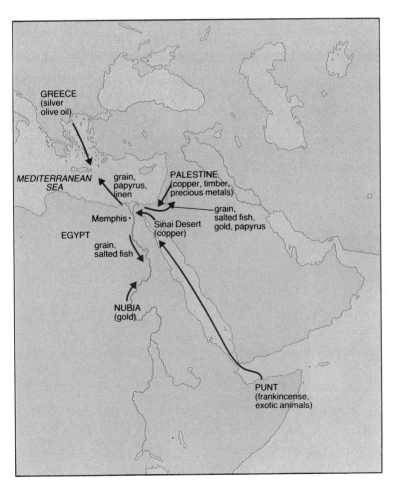

◁ **Trade with other countries.** Egypt had grain and salted fish which other countries needed – and gold, which they wanted. Much of the gold came from Nubia's northern region, where Egypt ruled for long periods. Other countries also wanted ropes and blank scrolls made from Egyptian papyrus. Egypt bartered these goods for things not found in the Nile Valley. Wood for making boats and furniture came from Palestine. Fragrant Palestinian cedar wood was especially in demand for tombs and temples. Copper also came from Palestine and from the Sinai Desert. Silver and olive oil came from Greece, and during the New Kingdom and late period many Greek traders settled in Memphis.

Travel and transport

The Egyptians made little use of two transport aids that were very important to other countries: the wheel and the camel. They could not use the wheel when building their great monuments, because of the sand. A wheel carrying a heavy weight across sand simply sinks. When dragging huge stones from the quarries to build pyramids or temples, the workers may have put round poles underneath for rollers, but they had no wagons. The Egyptians had no wheeled vehicles until the time of the **New Kingdom**, and then they used wheels only on war chariots. Even though these chariots were made light in weight, they could still sink into the sand. The only use made of the horse was to draw these chariots.

The camel was not used in Egypt until about 2000 years ago, 1000 years after it had already been put to work carrying people and loads in the Middle East. The donkey caravans that travelled to the oases in Egypt's western desert throughout most of Egypt's history could carry very little compared with a camel caravan. Isolated oases in the Middle East benefited much more from trade because the camel was a better pack animal.

△ **Still important today,** the donkey has been used for short local trips in Egypt, and for carrying burdens across the desert, for at least 5000 years. The donkey's wild ancestors lived only in Egypt and countries just south of Egypt, but many experts believe that it was the Mesopotamians, whose transportation problems were greater, who were the first to use this animal for work. Donkeys were not bred big enough to carry riders until the time of the Middle Kingdom.

◁ **Egypt's great advantage** was river transport. Boats could carry many times as much cargo as the pack animals that other countries relied on. The hieroglyphic sign for 'travelling south', even when the travel was by land, was a boat with sails, for the winds in Egypt normally blow from the north. The sign for 'travelling north' was a boat with oars. This boat of about 2400 years ago is using both oars and sails to go south with extra speed.

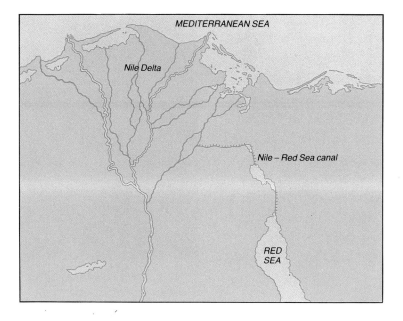

◁ **A canal from the Nile to the Red Sea** made trading expeditions to Africa and Arabia easier for later Egyptians. Begun by the pharaoh Necho II around 600BC, it was completed by the Persian emperor Darius in 490BC. It was about 85 kilometres long.

The Nile waterway

The Egyptians could survive well without the wheel or the camel because of their great river. The Nile provided a transport route that no other river could match. It carried almost everything and everyone needing to travel. The first barrier to boats on the Nile in those days before dams was the first **cataract**, the waterfall that formed the natural southern boundary of Egypt. The bottom of the cataract was only 85 metres above sea level. That meant there was only a gradual drop in the level of the land during the river's journey to the sea, and the current was very gentle.

In **predynastic** times the boats were all made of papyrus reeds. Later, wood from Palestine made it possible to build better boats. Some of these sailed along the coast to Palestine. Others went through the Red Sea and down the east coast of Africa as far as Somalia. However, throughout Egypt's history small papyrus boats continued to serve peasants and fishermen on local trips. Sails were of linen, tightly woven to make a heavy canvas.

The Old Kingdom

Egyptian history begins around 3100BC. This was when the Egyptians finally had enough symbols in their writing to record history. From this time, **inscriptions** and papyrus **scrolls** created a way for later Egyptians and for us to know about the past. It was also the time when the pharaoh Menes created Egypt by uniting the kingdoms of the Nile Valley and Nile Delta. He established Memphis in the north and Abydos in the south as his capital cities.

During about the first 400 years of Egyptian history, the **early period**, the first two **dynasties** of pharaohs came and went. They were barely able to hold Egypt together and stay in power. Lifestyle changed very

△ **The royal god Horus, the hawk,** sits behind the 4th-dynasty pharaoh Khephren (2520-2494BC?) in this symbolic statue representing the king's divine right to rule. This son of Khufu was one of the most powerful and successful pharaohs of the Old Kingdom.

The Great Pyramid of Khufu: statistics
Average weight of each block in the pyramid: 2.5 tons
Total number of blocks: 2 300 000
Years of Khufu's reign: 23 (2551 - 2528BC?)
Average number of blocks set in place each year of Khufu's reign: 100 000
Average number of blocks set in place each day of Khufu's reign: 285

◁ **The 4th-dynasty pyramids at Giza,** near modern-day Cairo, are the greatest pyramids of all Egyptian history. The largest is the Great Pyramid of Khufu (2551-2528BC?), a pharaoh remembered by the Egyptians as a tyrant who taxed the country mercilessly in order to build his monument.

little from **predynastic** times, and tombs and temples were still made mainly of mud bricks. Around 2649BC, however, there began a great age known as the **Old Kingdom**.

The first great age

The Old Kingdom lasted about 500 years. Its pharaohs belonged to the 3rd – 8th dynasties. Those of the 3rd and 4th dynasties were especially remarkable. They were the builders of the greatest pyramids, beginning with Zoser (2630-2611BC?), whose scribe Imhotep was regarded by later Egyptians as the father of architecture, sculpture and medicine.

Snofru (2575-2551BC?), the first pharaoh in the 4th dynasty, conquered part of northern Nubia, and built numerous temples and three small pyramids. His were the first **true pyramids**. Worship of the sun-god Re became especially important during his reign. Snofru was remembered as a good king by later generations, who worshipped him as a god. Two later pharaohs of the 4th dynasty, Khufu and his son Khephren, were remembered as selfish tyrants. However, they left remarkable monuments.

The 1st intermediate period

Later dynasties, however, lost control of northern Nubia. Egyptian power declined sharply as year upon year of low Nile floods left the country starving. The pharaohs had little power. Provincial governors, the **nomarchs**, ruled independently and passed on their offices to their sons by hereditary right. It was as though the country was ruled by many kings.

By about 2134BC the great age was truly over. This was the beginning of the 1st **intermediate period**, when different dynasties claimed to rule at the same time from different parts of the country.

△ **Zoser, greatest pharaoh of the 3rd dynasty,** for whom the first pyramid ever was built. The face of this statue of the pharaoh was battered thousands of years ago by thieves who stole the jewels originally set into the eyes. Egyptians 2500 years after Zoser's time still looked back on his reign as a golden age of outstanding achievement and wisdom.

The Middle Kingdom

The pharaohs of the southern **dynasty** which arose in Thebes during the 1st intermediate period — the 11th dynasty — were more able rulers than the northern pharaohs.

A pharaoh of the 11th dynasty called Mentuhotpe finally defeated the northern dynasty and reunited the country. He added to his name the title 'Uniter of the Two Lands' and proclaimed himself a god. It is from around 2040BC, during Mentuhotpe's reign in Thebes, that **Egyptologists** count the beginning of a new age in Egyptian history. It is called the Middle Kingdom, and it lasted about 400 years.

Founders of the 12th dynasty

The next two Middle Kingdom pharaohs, also called Mentuhotpe, ruled from Thebes. They revived the Red Sea trade route, which had not been used during the intermediate period, and opened new quarries as temple-building increased. The country became more prosperous. During this time, Amon, the god of the Thebans, became important throughout Egypt.

Somehow, the **vizier**, or prime minister, serving the last Mentuhotpe became pharaoh, founding the 12th dynasty. He was Amenhemhet I (1991-1962BC), who built a new capital city near Memphis, called Itjtawy, meaning 'Seizer of the Two Lands'.

Senwosret III

The 12th dynasty's fifth pharaoh, Senwosret III (1878-1841BC?), was the greatest king of the Middle Kingdom. He was one of the first pharaohs to keep a full-time army, and his military action both in Nubia and Palestine made Egypt very powerful. During his reign, the country's 42 small provinces or **nomes**, were abolished. The power of local nobles was reduced and the pharaoh's government became stronger.

△ **Senwosret I** (1971-1926BC?) with the god Ptah. During the early part of his reign, Senwosret ruled jointly with his father Amenhemet, the founder of the 12th dynasty. Under Amenhemet and Senwosret many fine stone buildings were constructed. Later generations had a great respect for the art and literature of this time.

The army of officials that Senwosret III created kept the country peaceful after his death. However, as officials gave themselves important titles and claimed more and more power in the districts where they governed, the pharaohs gradually became unimportant. One of them was Queen Nefrusobk (1787-1783BC?), the first woman to be pharaoh and the last pharaoh of the 12th dynasty. We know almost nothing about her.

The pharaohs that followed had little control over the country. They did not prevent Palestinian invaders from settling in the eastern part of the Nile Delta, and different dynasties began to rule from different parts of the country. After about 1640, the 15th dynasty, the **Hyksos**, who were invaders from Palestine, took over most of the country. This was the beginning of the 2nd intermediate period. The foreigners never managed to conquer the whole of Egypt. Native Egyptian pharoahs were able to control the south, ruling from their capital at Thebes.

△ **The most important pharaoh of the 12th dynasty,** Senwosret III posed for this unusual statue. Rather than giving the pharaoh perfection and youth, it shows the careworn face of an older man with oversized ears.

◁ **Amenhemhet III** (1844-1797BC?), who inherited the throne from Senwosret III, wore this gold breastplate with inlaid stones. It shows him, in a double image, destroying his enemies. In fact his long reign was a time of peace.

The New Kingdom

The **Hyksos** pharaohs of the 15th dynasty were in competition with two other dynasties. The first was the 16th dynasty who were also Hyksos. They held only a small territory in the Nile Delta. More important were the native Egyptian pharaohs of the 17th dynasty, who ruled from Thebes.

In the 1500s BC, the pharaohs ruling from Thebes began a struggle to expel the Hyksos from Egypt. Around 1550BC, a new dynasty, the 18th, took over in Thebes and completed the expulsion of the Hyksos around 1532BC. This was the beginning of the last great age of Egyptian history, the **New Kingdom**, which lasted for about 500 years.

The Egyptian empire

To expel the Hyksos, the Theban pharaohs had to master a new technology and new ways of fighting wars. The Hyksos had brought bronzeworking and ironworking to Egypt for the first time. They fought in horse-drawn chariots. Their weapons were better designed.

The Egyptians had to learn how to make chariots and weapons with the new metals. The Egyptians also had to learn how to use horses. The Thebans achieved all of this, and after winning the wars

△ **Amenhotep I** (1525-1504BC?), the second pharaoh of the 18th dynasty, pushed the Egyptian empire southwards into Nubia.

◁ **The two-wheeled horse-drawn war chariot** came to Egypt with the Hyksos during the 2nd intermediate period. The Egyptians had to learn to work iron and use horses before they could make their own chariots and fight in them against the Hyksos. They won their war against these invaders, and the New Kingdom began.

against the Hyksos, they were in charge of a united Egypt that stretched from northern Nubia to somewhere in Palestine.

The third pharaoh of the 18th dynasty, Thotmes I (1504-1492BC?), was the greatest conqueror in Egyptian history. He conquered Nubia, Palestine and Syria and kept them under Egyptian rule. The 18th dynasty also produced Hatshepsut (1473-1458BC?), the first powerful queen in history. The widow of Thotmes II, she began her rule as **regent** for her infant nephew, Thotmes III (1479-1425BC?). However, after seven years she proclaimed herself king. She dressed in a pharaoh's robes, and wore the pharaoh's ceremonial false beard.

Thotmes III did not take charge until she died, another 15 years later. He became very warlike and took back much land that had been lost since the time of Thotmes I.

The next three pharaohs of the 18th dynasty kept the empire strong. During the reign of Amenhotep III (1391-1353BC?) many of the greatest temples were built. The temples of Amon around Thebes flourished as pharaohs made enormous royal donations in thanks for military victories.

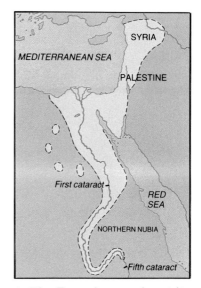

△ **The Egyptian empire at its peak,** under Thotmes I (1504-1492BC?).

◁ **The funerary temple of Queen Hatshepsut.** Funerary temples were looked after by priests following a great rulers death. The priests made offerings to the gods on behalf of the departed ruler's soul. Many years after her death, Hatshepsut's nephew Amenhotep III had all statues of her destroyed, and today we do not know what she looked like.

Akhnaton

T he **pharaoh** who inherited the throne of Egypt from Amenhotep III around 1353BC was known at first as Amenhotep IV. However, with his queen, Nefertiti, he started a new religion in Egypt, and this inspired him to change his name. The new religion was a worship of the sun-god under the name Aton, meaning 'sun disc'. The pharaoh's name became 'Akhnaton', meaning 'beneficial to the sun-disc'.

The new religion

Akhnaton wanted the Egyptians to worship only Aton, and he eventually closed the temples of all other gods. The word 'gods' in the plural was hacked out of inscriptions with chisels. The name of the god Amon, who had made the priests of Thebes wealthy and powerful, in particular was attacked with chisels. For this, Akhnaton's religion was much hated by these priests.

At the time when he changed his name, Akhnaton abandoned Thebes as his capital and built a new one, Akhtaton, at a place now called el'Amarna, half way between Memphis and Thebes. At its centre was a roofless temple, open to the sun. While the capital

△ **Family resemblance.**
Akhnaton's queen, Nefertiti, looks from this sculpture to have been the most beautiful woman in Egyptian history.

In reliefs her husband appears deformed, as in the one below. His daughters are also shown with unusual heads, as in the painting on the left. Many historians have wondered if they had an hereditary illness.

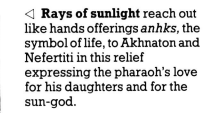

◁ **Rays of sunlight** reach out like hands offerings *anhks,* the symbol of life, to Akhnaton and Nefertiti in this relief expressing the pharaoh's love for his daughters and for the sun-god.

was at el'Amarna, a new and different style of painting and sculpture began. This is called the **Amarna period** in Egyptian art. The new style was highly realistic. People's faces showed more expression, and great care was taken to record individual features. Amarna art was very unlike traditional Egyptian art, which had always shown unreal pictures of people as they were expected to appear after perfection in the afterlife.

Nefertiti probably had a lot of influence on Akhnaton's ideas and decisions. Before he died, the name of a joint ruler, Nefernefruaton (probably Nefertiti), began to appear in his inscriptions.

The last days of empire

During Akhnaton's rule Egypt's enemies became stronger. The Hittites, a warlike people from what is today Turkey, took Syria from Egypt. Many Egyptians were afraid that this was a sign of anger from the old gods. The nobles and the army remembered that when they had worshipped Amon rather than Aton, they had always had victories.

Soon after Akhnaton died, the pharaoh was the boy king Tutankhaton, probably the son of a minor wife of Aknhaton, married to a daughter of Nefertiti. Tutankhaton's guardians were Aya, who had been Akhnaton's **vizier**, and Haremhab, who had been his chief general. They judged it best to move the capital to Memphis and to change the new young **pharaoh's** name from Tutankhaton to Tutankhamon, to honour the old god Amon.

The 19th dynasty

Aya became pharaoh when Tutankhamon died, then Haremhab took the throne, founding the 19th **dynasty**. The second pharaoh in the 19th dynasty was Seti I (1305-1290BC?). Seti fought many battles with the Hittites and regained some of the lost territory in Syria.

Rameses II (1290-1224BC?) fought the Hittites to a standstill in southern Syria and made a peace with them that lasted for about 50 years. He married several Hittite princesses during his long reign of 66 years, in order to create friendly relations with the Hittite royal family.

Later pharaohs had to fight off Libyan invaders from the west, and the 'sea peoples'. These were several waves of invaders who came from a land somewhere on the shores of the Mediterranean. Historians have not been able to identify where. The 19th dynasty died out following the brief reign of Queen Twosre (1198-1196BC?).

△ **The last pharaoh of the 18th dynasty,** Tutankhamon, died young. When his advisors abandoned Akhnaton's worship of Aton and returned to the worship of Amon, the young king gave up his original name: Tutankhaton. He is famous because the wonderful riches left in his tomb were never taken by robbers and we can see them in museums today.

The 20th dynasty

The last Egyptian king to hold much territory in Palestine was the 20th-dynasty pharaoh Rameses III (1194-1163BC?). After him, Egypt gradually lost control of land in the Middle East. Some time during this dynasty, historians believe that the biblical Hebrews left Egypt to make their own homeland in Palestine. Egypt also lost control of Nubia.

The pharaohs gradually lost power to the priests. Tax records show that more and more property was owned by the temples. The priestly offices became hereditary, and eventually the priests of Thebes ruled **Upper Egypt** independently. Egypt entered its 3rd **intermediate period** around 1070BC, with the coming of the 21st dynasty, which controlled only the Nile Delta.

△ **Seti I** receiving from the god Horus the crook and flail, which stood for royal authority. The first important pharaoh of the 19th dynasty, he destroyed Akhnaton's city of Akhtaton and removed Akhnaton's name from inscriptions all over the country.

◁ **Rameses II.** Later Egyptians thought he must have been the greatest of all kings, because he built more temples and more enormous statues of himself than any other pharaoh in history. The country actually became poorer during his reign of 66 years. He had hundreds of wives and over 900 children.

Foreign rule

After the **New Kingdom** crumbled, Egypt remained divided for more than 700 years. Meanwhile the countries of the Middle East were growing stronger. Egypt had little iron, but other countries began to equip common soldiers with iron weapons and ordinary farmers with iron tools. The camel was tamed, and camel caravans were used to move Middle Eastern goods more efficiently.

Nubia too, grew strong, because of the gold in its northern region, which the Egyptians no longer controlled. Around 770BC, Nubian kings took control of southern Egypt and made it part of Nubia. These were the pharaohs of the 25th dynasty.

The late period

Shabaka (712-698BC?), a Nubian king of the 25th dynasty, conquered the whole of Egypt. This was the start of the **late period**, a phase lasting more than 300 years when the country was united. However, during this phase, there were only a few times when the country was ruled by a native Egyptian. Assyria, a new empire in the Middle East, invaded Egypt twice during the reign of the Nubian Taharka (690-640BC?).

◁ **Cleopatra and her son Caesarion,** with whom she ruled jointly over Egypt, making offerings to the Egyptian goddess Hathor. This relief appears on the wall of the temple of Hathor in Alexandria. For over 300 years, Greek-speaking pharaohs, including Queen Cleopatra, ruled Egypt from their city of Alexandria in Lower Egypt, which became a world centre of Greek culture.

◁ **A mixture of cultures.** This Egyptian mummy case of around AD100 bears a very un-Egyptian picture of the young Roman encased inside. Named Artemidorus, he died at about the age of 20. The Romans took control of Egypt from the Greek pharaohs in 30BC. Over the next 700 years Egypt's style of art and religion were abandoned as the Egyptians became Christian. Arabs invaded in AD640 and began converting the Egyptians to the Islamic religion. Today Egyptians speak Arabic.

The Egyptians took advantage of this to fight against the Nubians. An Egyptian pharaoh drove out the Nubians in 664BC, and his dynasty ruled for almost 150 years.

Persia seized Egypt in 525BC. The Egyptians revolted and managed to keep foreigners out between 404BC and 343BC, when the Persians returned. The Persians were finally replaced by the Greek conqueror Alexander the Great in 332BC and the late period was followed by the **Greek period**. In 30BC, Egypt became a province of Rome.

Time line

60

BC

5000?
The wet climate following the last Ice Age is at its peak

5000 - 3100?
The predynastic period. As the valley becomes less swampy, the Egyptians move from hunting and gathering first to part-time, then full-time farming. Craftsmanship with stone, copper, clay, wood and leather. The Egyptians trade with each other using papyrus boats on the Nile. Several kingdoms rule different parts of the river. Early forms of hieroglyphic writing are scratched onto stones

3100?
By warfare, Menes becomes the first pharaoh of all Egypt. Hieroglyphic writing begins to record Egyptian history

3100 - 2649?
The early period. 1st - 2nd dynasties control the country from a capital at Memphis. Trade with Palestine and Nubia

2649?
Beginning of the Old Kingdom (3rd - 8th dynasties)

2630 -2611?
Reign of Zoser. Construction of the Step Pyramid

2575 - 2465?
The 4th dynasty, the age of the true pyramids. Conquest of northern Nubia

2134?
End of the Old Kingdom. Egypt breaks up into different parts, as poor harvests lead to the 1st intermediate period (the 9th - 11th dynasties rule different parts of Egypt at the same time)

2040?
Mentuhotpe, with his capital at Thebes, brings the different parts of Egypt together again and establishes the Middle Kingdom (11th - 14th dynasties)

1991 - 1783?
The 12th dynasty, with a capital at Itjtawy near Memphis. Northern Nubia reconquered. Military expeditions to Palestine

1640?
End of the Middle Kingdom as Hyksos invaders from Palestine establish a 15th dynasty. Beginning of 2nd intermediate period, with 15th and 17th dynasties ruling parts of the country, but dominated by the Hyksos. Hyksos introduce the horse and chariot, bronze- and ironworking

1550?
Beginning of the New Kingdom, as the 18th dynasty, with a capital in Thebes, drives out Hyksos and brings Egypt together. Northern Nubia reconquered. Parts of Palestine conquered

1504 - 1492?	Thotmes I creates the Egyptian empire by moving further into Nubia and conquering Palestine and Syria
1473 - 1458?	Hatshepsut, first queen to rule with full royal power
1391 - 1353	Under Amenhotep III, the Egyptian empire is at its peak
1353 - 1335?	Akhnaton builds new capital at Akhtaton (el'Amarna) and forces Egyptians to worship only the sun-god Aton. Beginning of realistic Amarna period in Egyptian art
1333 - 1323?	Tutankhamon, last pharaoh of the 18th dynasty. His advisors move capital to Memphis and restore old religion. Amarna period ends
1307 - 1070?	19th - 20th dynasties. Several pharaohs called Rameses build impressive monuments, but Egypt loses control of land in Palestine and Nubia
1070?	End of the New Kingdom as the priests of Thebes begin ruling Upper Egypt themselves. Beginning of 3rd intermediate period (21st - 25th dynasties)
770?	The Nubians conquer most of Upper Egypt. Their kings become the 25th dynasty

712?	Beginning of the late period (25th - 31st dynasties), as the Nubians conquer the rest of Egypt
671 - 673	The Assyrians seize Egypt from the Nubians, who take it back
664	Necho I drives out the Nubians and makes Egypt independent
525	The Persians conquer Egypt
404 - 343	The Egyptians drive the Persians out for 70 years
343 - 332	The Persians rule Egypt again
332	Alexander the Great of Macedon, Greece, seizes Egypt from the Persians and founds the Greek-speaking city of Alexandria
332 - 30	Greek period, with Greek-speaking pharaohs
30	Egypt becomes a province of the Roman empire
AD 394	Last inscription in hieroglyphics. Egypt almost wholly Christian
640	The Arabs conquer Egypt. They begin to settle in the country and to convert the Egyptians to the Islamic religion. Only a Christian minority (Copts) keep the Egyptian language, and only for religious services

Glossary

absolute ruler: a king whose power to govern is not limited by law

afterlife: the life of the body's soul after death

akhet: the season of the Nile flood, August to October

Amarna period: the brief period in Egyptian art when sculptures and paintings were very different and more realistic than traditional Egyptian art. The period began under the pharaoh Akhnaton and ended shortly after his death

anatomy: the study of human bodies

archaeologist: a person who tries to work out what happened in the past by finding and studying old buildings and objects

ba: the part of a body's soul that the Egyptians believed could travel to the Underworld

barter: to trade or bargain with goods

cartouche: in hieroglyphics, an oval frame with a bar at one end, enclosing the pharaoh's two most important names: his birth name and a name praising the sun-god Re

cataract: a large waterfall that prevented boats from passing

civilization: a large group of people who have settled in one place and live in the same organized way. They follow the same customs, and produce their own style in art

deben: weights used by traders to value goods such as a sack of grain

delta: the fan-shaped area of muddy land at the place where a river divides and flows into the sea

demotic script: a simplified form of the ancient Egyptian hieratic script. It was used between 700BC and AD450

dynasty: a line of rulers belonging to the same family

early period: the time of the 1st and 2nd Egyptian dynasties (3100-2649BC?)

Egyptologist: an expert who studies ancient Egypt

excavation: the careful digging up of buried objects to find information about the past

Greek period: the time following Alexander the Great's conquest, when the pharaohs spoke Greek and Alexandria became the main centre of Greek civilization (332-30BC)

hieratic script: a simplified form of Egyptian writing which first appeared during the early period

hieroglyphics: a Greek word for an elaborate form of Egyptian writing used for formal messages like inscriptions. It used both pictures and sound signs

hunter-gatherers: people who live by hunting for game, and gathering plant food

Hyksos: the people who invaded Egypt from Palestine, and ruled Egypt during the 15th and 16th dynasties

inscription: a formal message set down in an especially long-lasting form, eg carved in stone

intermediate period: the period when Egypt was divided between two or more rival dynasties. There were three of these periods.

irrigation: a system of watering crops by channelling water from a river along pipes or ditches

ka: the body-spirit that the Egyptians believed could not survive unless the dead person's body was mummified

kilt: a knee-length skirt worn by men

late period: a time of unity but of foreign domination (712?-332BC) following the 3rd intermediate period

linen: a strong cloth made from the fibres of the flax plant

Lower Egypt: the part of Egypt that included the Nile Delta and the Nile Valley as far south as Memphis

mastaba: a tomb made of mud bricks and stone in the predynastic or early period

Middle Kingdom: the second great age in Egypt (2040-1640BC?)

mummy: a body preserved by drying

New Kingdom: the last great age in Egypt (1550-1070BC?), including the days of the Egyptian Empire

nomarch: the Greek word for the governor of a nome

nome: the Greek word for a small Egyptian province. Egypt was divided into 42 nomes, until they were abolished during the Middle Kingdom

oasis: an isolated, fertile area in a dry region where crops can be grown

Old Kingdom: the first great age in Egypt (2649-2134BC?) when most of the pyramids were built

papyrus: a reed which grew in Nile swamps. The shoots were a luxury food. The stems were woven together to make boats. The pith was cut into strips which stuck together when beaten. These papyrus sheets were used to write on

peret: the season of planting and fresh growth from November to February

pharoah: a king of Egypt

polygamy: a marriage in which either there is more than one wife, or more than one husband

predynastic period: the time before Egyptian history began

prehistoric: describes the times before there were any written records

regent: someone who rules the country on behalf of a child who is too young to inherit the throne

relief: a picture carved in a flat surface

scribe: an official, a secretary or a clerk whose work involved writing

scroll: several sheets of papyrus joined into a rolled strip

shemu: the dry season from March to August when crops ripened and were harvested

shrine: a holy place where believers keep an object that they closely link with a god or spirit

step pyramid: a tomb or temple built up of layers, each smaller than the one below

true pyramid: a tomb or temple with a square base and four outside walls in the form of triangles that meet at the top

Underworld: the world of the afterlife, where the Egyptians believed that the sun-god came back to life each night

Upper Egypt: the part of Egypt that included the Nile Valley from Memphis south to the first cataract

vizier: an Arabic word for the scribe who was the chief advisor to the pharaoh

Index